Knowing Christ

Craig McCourt

Interior design by GodPonders Publishing

First Published in 2016 by GodPonders Publishing

ISBN: 0692616640
ISBN-13: 978-0692616642 (GodPonders Publishing)

DEDICATION

To my sons Isaiah Paul and Noah John, my desire and
prayer for their life is nothing more than for them both
to **Know Christ**!

CONTENTS

ACKNOWLEDGMENTS

There have been so many godly men who have poured into my life over the past 50+ years. I have had the privilege of gathering with them around dining room tables, in youth rooms, around fire pits, and even in hospital rooms as together we have grown to Know Christ more. These men have shaped my great love for being a student of the Word.

My love for teaching the Word comes from 25+ years gathering with thousands of youth and adults, and sharing the Word of Life with them. Their questions and insightful faith have helped to shape the teacher I am today.

Special thanks to the men's Bible study group at St. Michael's Lutheran Church in Bloomington, who helped take the rough edges off this study.

1
KNOWING

*17 I keep asking that the God of our Lord Jesus Christ,
the glorious Father, may give you the Spirit of wisdom and revelation,
so that you may know him better.*
Ephesians 1:17 (NIV)

Let's be honest: getting to know someone these days can be quite difficult. In this age of information, it only takes a few clicks of the mouse to know quite a bit about someone. We can know where they were born, where they went to school, who they married, all the places they have called home over the last 30 years, all the photos of poor choices they posted on Facebook . . . yet still we will not really know them.

Knowing someone can truly only come when we spend time with them—significant time with them. My wife Shirley and I met one summer while serving together on staff at a Christian camp in Wisconsin.

That summer was spent together. By day, we worked in the camp office together. We lived in the "staff dorm," so we even shared the same staff lounge in our free time. There was no doubt, we spent a lot of time together.

By the end of the summer, we were beginning to know each other pretty well. So well, in fact, that by October of that same first year, I asked her to marry me. To many that seems "quick," but we had spent serious time together, getting to know one another.

When you spend time together, you get past the façade that we all put up, and you begin to discover the "real person." That is where the value in a relationship begins— when we move beyond the surface to the reality below.

1) Think of a fellow employee or neighbor— someone who it has taken time to get to "really" know. What types of things have you learned about them over time?

2) Is it possible to get to know someone without spending time with them? Explain your answer.

Early in our nation's history, we faced a serious problem. Counterfeiting currency was becoming a huge issue. The

American public's confidence in our nation's currency was wavering. In 1865, the United States Secret Service was formed to deter the rise of counterfeiters.

Shortly after that, in 1869, the Bureau of Engraving and Printing began to be the only location for printing currency. Ever since those days, our nation's currency has been under almost constant revision and improvement. From security threads to micro-printing and well-guarded ink formulations, our currency ranks among the most difficult to counterfeit in the world.

It still happens, though; counterfeit U.S. currency is still an issue. The Secret Service is still hot on the trail of those who counterfeit currency. For as often as the average person handles a dollar bill, how well do you think you could spot a fraud? Do you know the things to check for when taking a $100 bill in a transaction?

3) Take two minutes and, on your own in the boxes below, fill in the major layout design elements of a $5 bill. Include the following:
- Portrait (who is it?)
- Treasury seal
- Serial number
- In God We Trust
- Denomination Number (i.e. 5)
- Country designation
- What image is on the back?

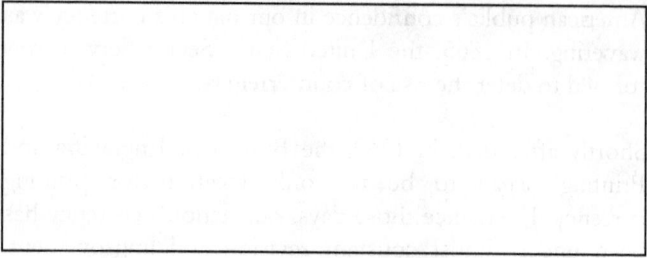

Front of a U.S. $5 bill

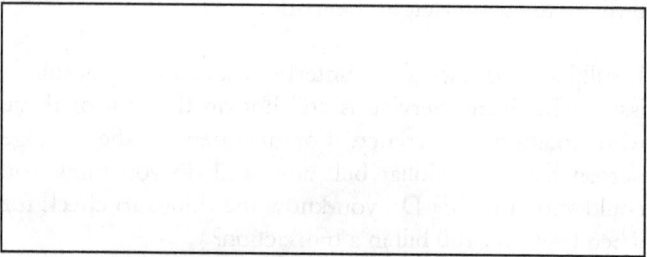

Back of a U.S. $5 bill

4) Hopefully there is someone in your group with a $5 bill and you can compare your layout with that of the "real thing." Take a moment and see how you did. What features did you get right? What did you totally get wrong?

5) What would you do if I told you next week we were going to test your knowledge of a $10 bill?

The Secret Service agents do not study counterfeit money to know all the flaws to look for. They study the real thing so that, by knowing the bill so well in every detail, they can spot a counterfeit easily. That is my desire for this study as well: that you would grow to know Christ so well that you can easily spot a counterfeit.

6) Read *Exodus 33:12–23*. Why does Moses ask to be taught the ways of God (v. 13)?

7) What other request does Moses bring to the Lord in verse 18?

8) How does the Lord answer this request? What caution does He give Moses in verse 20?

9) Moses comes down from the mountain after spending 40 days with the Lord. What is different about Moses when he returns to the people? (read *Exodus 34:29–30*)

10) What happens to us as a result of spending time with the Lord?

Read *Philippians 3:7–10*

11) What things get in the way of you knowing Christ more fully?

Forgive me for getting personal, but if your group is like most, the answer to question 11 is nothing more than a series of excuses. We still need to get at the deeper issue of what is keeping us from knowing Christ. Is it fear—that others will think I'm strange for spending so much time on it? Am I afraid that if I know Christ more, He will demand more of me than I want to give? Is it the idea that I do know the facts of the life of Christ, so what else is there to know?

12) Sometimes we are plagued by the idea of giving something up in our pursuit of Knowing Christ. What are you willing to give up to know Christ more?

PRAYER

Jesus, stir up your strong Spirit within us that we might desire to Know You above all things. Remove from us the distractions and counterfeits that fill our world and help our lives reflect the glory of your presence. Amen.

FOR NEXT WEEK

To prepare for our study of Colossians, take 15 minutes and read through the four chapters of Colossians. As you read, look for a verse or two that stand out to you as a new idea, a key reminder, or a puzzling thought. Write out those verses here, with a few words to remind yourself why you chose them.

MEMORY CHALLENGE

10 I want to know Christ and the power of his resurrection and the fellowship of sharing in his sufferings, becoming like him in his death, 11 and so, somehow, to attain to the resurrection from the dead.

Philippians 3:10–11 (NIV)

2
PAUL AND COLOSSAE

¹ Paul, an apostle of Christ Jesus by the will of God, and Timothy our brother, ² To the holy and faithful brothers in Christ at Colosse: Grace and peace to you from God our Father.
Colossians 1:1–2 (NIV)

I grew up in Wisconsin, and my loyalty to the Green Bay Packers is in my DNA. (I hope this does not cause any of you to walk away from the study at this point. I will try to keep my Packers illustrations to a minimum.)

While I didn't go to my first regular season game at Lambeau Feld until I was 50 years old, I have been a fan as long as I can remember. As a child, I grew up with the likes of Bart Starr and Ray Nitschke.

When I was about ten, a neighbor took his grandson Marc and I to the Packers' practice camp in Green Bay. I was amazed at how big those guys were as I watched them walk past me on their way to the field.

Many years later when I was in college, my roommate Ray took me to his home in Green Bay one Sunday and I was introduced to his neighbor, "Ray Nitschke" . . . I still remember what an honor it was to meet him and how much I hoped, when he finished shaking my hand, that I would get all my fingers back.

    1)   Have you had a brush with fame? What famous person did you meet or catch a glimpse of?

When Colossians was first written, it was a letter. (You remember those—they were one or more sheets of paper with words on them put there by a pen in someone's hand.) In this case, the letter was written by Paul and sent to the church in Colossae.

Paul wrote 13 total letters to churches, and those letters have survived to this day in the Holy Bible. Colossians is one of only two of those thirteen letters that Paul wrote that went to a church he had not founded. The other letter as such was Romans. Most of the members of the church in Colossae had never met Paul.

What a thrill it must have been for them to hear from the Apostle Paul. Because Paul had spent three years in Ephesus (in the same Roman province as Colossae), he was well-known throughout the region and stories of his powerful teaching were spreading far and wide.

    2)   What Christian leader today would you feel honored and excited to get a personal letter from?

As we study Colossians, read it with the excitement and anticipation that the first recipients would have enjoyed. It is a personal letter written from God, through Paul, to you and me and the church on Earth today. It doesn't get much better than that.

COLOSSAE – Some Background

Colossae was 100 miles east of Ephesus on the Lycus River in what is modern Turkey. While the nearby city of Laodicea may have been a more influential city, Colossae was at a crossroads and was a trading center for ideas and religions. Many Jews from Jerusalem fled to Colossae under the persecutions of Antiochus III and IV. This was almost 200 years before Christ. At the time of Paul, the Jewish population of the area was large.

Colossae was also home of great diversity, both culturally and religiously. Like so much of the region, the worship of idols and paganism abounded. Christians were, at the time of this letter, certainly in a minority in Colossae. This brought with it no shortage of opportunity to water down their faith or to adapt it to be more "favorable" to the people of the area.

We have no reason to believe that Paul ever spent time in Colossae. While he may have passed through the city on his third missionary journey, he did not stop and do ministry there. So what is Paul's connection to the city? Epaphras (1:7) was a convert of Paul's and the founder of the church in Colossae. Despite Paul's lack of ministry there, he was certainly not disconnected from their faith and their struggles.

Read *Colossians 1:1–2*

3) How does Paul introduce himself? How does he address the recipients of the letter?

Read *Colossians 3:1–11*

4) How does this contrast with the greeting in Colossians 1:2? How would he write his greeting to your study group?

Read *Colossians 1:1–8*

5) What characteristics of the Colossians led Paul to share words of thanks for them?

6) What is the source of their faith? (vs. 6–8)

7) What do we learn about Epaphras in these verses? What trait of the Colossians does Epaphras single out as he speaks to Paul?

8) How do you feel when someone tells you about something they notice or appreciate in you?

Read *Colossians 1:9–14*

9) What specifics does Paul pray for the Colossians?

The focus of this study comes from verse 9. Biblical knowledge is, as we covered in lesson one, more than just the possession of facts. Knowing Christ is so much more about how we "do life." We will look at what it means to live a godly life and bear fruit in a broken world. Part of that godly life we live is a life of prayer.

How many times have you been asked by a study member or friend at church to pray for them or a member of their family? As you go about your day, and a friend or family member comes to mind, do you lift up a quick, "God, bless Greg today." If so, what are you praying for? How will you know if your prayer was ever answered?

10) How might this prayer of Paul's (vs. 9–11) serve as a model for your prayers?

Read *Ephesians 1:15–23*

11) What common practice of Paul do these verses show us? How can you incorporate this model into your daily prayer life?

As you look at the other people in this study, what are your desires for them? If you could share a daily prayer for them, what would your prayer look like? Write it out inside the back cover of this book and use it as a prayer for your group throughout the rest of this study.

PRAYER

Lord, we come rejoicing that you have written this letter to us—what an honor to hear from you. Fill us with more of you, that we might know you and through that knowledge of you see your will for our lives. Help us to be encouragers of those around us, as we acknowledge your gifts at work in their lives. Guide us to pray deeply and specifically for those people you place on our hearts this week. Amen.

FOR NEXT WEEK

To prepare for our study next week, read through the creation account in Genesis 1 and 2. After reading, write a short 2–3 sentence summary of the account.

MEMORY CHALLENGE

[13] *For he has rescued us from the dominion of darkness and brought us into the kingdom of the Son he loves,* [14] *in whom we have redemption, the forgiveness of sins.*

Colossians 1:13–14 (NIV)

3
SUFFICIENCY OF CHRIST

18 And he is the head of the body, the church;
he is the beginning and the firstborn from among the dead,
so that in everything he might have the supremacy.
Colossians 1:18 (NIV)

It might seem like an odd statement to make, but I believe that there are few people in the church who truly question the "supremacy of Christ." From the ancient creeds we pronounce that He is God of Gods, and Lord of Lords. Our worship songs declare Him to be the King of Kings, and the Ancient of Days. We speak of Him as the unchallenged creator of heaven and earth, and the master keeper of creation.

I believe we struggle when it comes to recognizing the "sufficiency of Christ." The simple idea that we do not need to add anything to who He is or what He has done, in order to make our life complete. I often find people working very hard to "add" to the work that Christ has done in their life to reach the point where they feel fully redeemed.

Often people are plagued by the feeling that the sacrifice of Jesus now allows God to tolerate them. They see the many sins of their life as a huge hole from which they need to climb out of in order to move from being tolerated to being loved.

They work hard to be a good spouse and friend. They struggle at even the slighted slip in their behavior and see it as a mortal failure . The stress of the life they try to lead, a life worthy of God's love, become a huge burden for them to carry around. The miss the joy of their salvation.

This also can be seen in our culture of "more and better." Contentment seems to be something we search after, but it is just out of reach. On my many mission trips to places that are home to some of the world's most impoverished people, I have seen the elusive contentment in the hearts and on the faces of saints, who in this life appear to have nothing. They have discovered the sufficiency of Christ.

1) How do you find yourself struggling with contentment?

For many years, I sent out a daily email devotion for men. I would often hear from subscribers about a topic that seems to hit close to home for them—contentment. Today as we look at the supremacy of Christ, I pray you see in His supremacy, His great sufficiency also.

"All roads lead to God" or "We are all working to get to the same place" are common sentiments these days. Even the Colossians heard this message, "It's good to worship

Jesus, but not exclusively." Jesus was viewed as one among many spirits worthy of praise. Paul addresses this false idea head-on.

Read *Colossians 1:1–23*

2) How does recognizing the supremacy of Christ help you to understand the simple fact of Jesus being the only way to the Father?

3) What difficulty do you have in relating to an invisible God?

4) The writer to the Hebrews states, "The Son is the radiance of God's glory, and the exact representation of his being"(Hebrews 1:3). Couple this with John's words, "No one has ever seen God, but God the One and Only who is at the Father's side, has made him known" (John 1:18) and Paul's description of Christ in verse 15. How do these verses help overcome the difficulty of an invisible God?

5) From these verses, how would you answer someone who asks, "How can I get to know God?"

6) From verses 15-18, create a list of truths you know about the supremacy of Christ. Begin each statement with "Christ is…"

7) Modern optics, from microscopes to telescopes, have helped us to see creation like never before. We have seen the detailed workings of a single cell, and peered into the vast unnumbered galaxies of our universe. How does this add to your understanding of the supremacy of Christ over creation?

Read *Colossians 1:18–20*

8) Christ is given the title of "the head of the body of Christ, the church." How is the headship of Christ seen in your church? Where might it be lacking?

9) The firstborn in the culture of Jesus' day was given special rights and privileges. What does it mean to you that Christ is the firstborn from among the dead?

10) Jesus is called our reconciliation. What does it mean to reconcile something?

Read *Colossians 1:21–23*

11) What had separated the Colossians from Christ? How has He now reconciled them?

12) What challenge does Paul place before the Colossians (v. 23)? How does this challenge apply to you?

13) What does it mean to you to be "without blemish and free from accusation"?

14) How does our growing understanding of Jesus' supremacy over "creation"(v.15), "authority"(v. 16), "the church" (v. 18), and "death" (v. 19) help you to understand the sufficiency of Christ in your life?

15) Why does Paul stress his connection to the gospel as one of a servant? How would you describe your relationship with the gospel?

PRAYER

Heavenly Father, it is so very hard for us to grasp the nature of the Trinity. It is just as difficult for us to grasp the love of Christ, who is supreme over all things, yet He would willingly take on my sin and die for me. Help me to recognize daily the amazing gift given to me in the gospel, and allow me to be a faithful steward of that same gospel. Amen.

FOR NEXT WEEK

Based on your knowledge of Christ, write a summary of who Christ is that you could share with someone who wants to know more.

MEMORY CHALLENGE

21 Once you were alienated from God and were enemies in your minds because of your evil behavior. 22 But now he has reconciled you by Christ's physical body through death to present you holy in his sight, without blemish and free from accusation.
Colossians 1:21–22 (NIV)

4
GOSPEL SERVANT

*25 I have become its servant by the commission God gave me to
present to you the word of God in its fullness.*
Colossians 1:25 (NIV)

You don't have to read much of Paul's writings in the New
Testament to recognize him as a glass-half-full kind of guy.
A theme that runs throughout his writings is one of
grateful rejoicing. Paul writes to the Philippians,

*"I know what it is to be in need, and I know what it is to have
plenty. I have learned the secret of being content in any and every
situation, whether well fed or hungry, whether living in plenty or in
want."* **Philippians 4:12**

What is Paul's secret? It is to rejoice! Not just when the
praise band is leading the charge on a Sunday morning, but
also when you are stuck in traffic on your commute home.
In Paul's case, it was to rejoice while being held against his
will under house arrest in Rome. Unable to move about as
he would like, Paul was restricted in what he could do in
fulfilling his Apostolic call.

Paul identified himself as a servant of the gospel,

> *"Paul, a servant of Christ Jesus, called to be an apostle and set apart for the gospel of God"* **Romans 1:1**

> *"I became a servant of this gospel by the gift of God's grace given me through the working of his power."* **Ephesians 3:7**

He tells the believers in Colossae that he has suffered for them.

> *Now I rejoice in what was suffered for you, and I fill up in my flesh what is still lacking in regard to Christ's afflictions, for the sake of his body, which is the church.* **Colossians 1:24**

He shares with them about the amazing mystery of God's love in Christ that Paul has been privileged to share. He also prays for them and for the church of Laodicea.

1) In what situations do you find it difficult to rejoice? When do you find it easy?

2) Is "rejoicing" something you think about on a daily basis? If not, how might you ponder rejoicing more often?

Read *Colossians 1:24*

3) For whom does Paul see himself suffering?

4) Is it easier to suffer for a noble cause? What goal in your life have you been willing to suffer to achieve?

Read *Colossians 1:25–2:1*

5) How does Paul define the commission given to him?

6) When the Bible talks about a mystery, it is not talking about something we would call mysterious. It is talking about something hidden that has been revealed by God in His time. How does Paul define the "glorious riches of this mystery"?

7) How might the gospel of Christ be considered a "mystery"?

8) Read Colossians 2:4, 8. In light of their struggles, outlined in these verses, why might Paul have chosen to describe the gospel as a mystery?

9) Where does Paul find his strength to labor and struggle for the sake of the gospel? (vs. 28-29)

10) List some real-life examples of ways that you gain strength for the labors of the day.

Read **Colossians 2:2–5**

11) What are Paul's purposes for serving as outlined in these verses?

12) In the context of the local church, the body of Christ, what is the obligation of the pastor to the people he serves?

13) As a lay member of the congregation, what is your role in ministry to your pastor?

14) Paul talks about suffering for the gospel. Do you have any personal experience in suffering for the sake of the gospel? If so, do you, like Paul, find joy in the suffering?

15) What can you do this week to encourage those who lead ministry at your church? How can you carry this work out beyond this week?

PRAYER

We thank you for the mystery revealed to us in the life, death and resurrection of Jesus. Help us to be willing to live and serve the gospel, regardless of the personal cost. Remind us to lift up our pastors and church leaders as we encourage and support them in their work for the gospel. Continue to draw us into a deeper relationship with you in the days and weeks ahead in this study. Amen.

FOR NEXT WEEK

Reread the book of Colossians again, listening for the voice of a pastor for his people. Find the one verse that most encourages you for the week and write it below.

MEMORY CHALLENGE

28 We proclaim him, admonishing and teaching everyone with all wisdom, so that we may present everyone perfect in Christ.

Colossians 1:28 (NIV)

5
ROOTS

⁶ So then, just as you received Christ Jesus as Lord,
continue to live in him,
⁷ rooted and built up in him,
strengthened in the faith as you were taught,
and overflowing with thankfulness.
Colossians 2:6–7 (NIV)

Next time you are playing a trivia game and the question is, "What kind of tree has the deepest roots?" Answer with great confidence, "a wild fig tree at Echo Caves, in South Africa." In fact, the roots of this tree measure 400 feet deep into the ground, according to the *Guinness Book of Records*.

Closer to home, when we are looking for a tree with deep roots, we need look no further than the mighty oak tree. Long known for its stability and strength, the oak is a tree that often stands the test of time. This does not come as quick growth, however.

I still remember the day when our son Isaiah returned home one day from 1st grade, proudly bearing an oak sapling. He could hardly wait to get it in the ground. His teacher had informed the class that oak trees make great climbing trees . . . and what little boy doesn't want a good climbing tree in his yard? I hated to be the one who told him it would be his grandchildren that would likely be climbing any oak tree he planted.

Developing deep roots is important for the life of a tree. Since most trees are planted outdoors, they must face the harsh reality of the weather. From violent winds to driving rains, many trees fight to survive in harsh conditions. Trees are also forced to grow tall to allow their canopy of leaves to rise above the others if they are to survive and thrive.

Paul talks to the Colossian Christians about being rooted in Christ. They were a new church planted with great joy. Imagine the image of a grove of young trees, all planted to the same starting depth. Paul now encourages these young trees to continue to grow and to get stronger. Paul knows the challenges that will come against these believers. He knows well about the suffering and false teaching that will challenge their faith and their ability to stand.

Read *Colossians 2:6–7*

1) Look back at Colossians 1:6. What is another reason that Paul wants these believers to continue growing deep?

As a church worker, I have lived in many different states. Some of these locations we have lived in longer than others. I have discovered over the years that the longer you stay somewhere, the harder it is to leave. Why is that? We are often said to have "put down roots." Think about the roots you have put down in your life—from family and friends, to clubs and organizations. Many times we feel rooted around our children, their schools, and their activities.

2) In the space below, list some of the ways you have become rooted in your life. List some of the benefits and nourishment that comes from these rootings in your life.

a.

b.

c.

3) How rooted are you with the people of this study? What can make it difficult to go deep in a group? What can make it easier?

4) Can you think of a time in your life when your roots of faith felt like they were just below the surface?

5) Can you think of a time when you could almost feel your roots of faith growing deeper? If someone were looking into your life from the outside, what might they have seen during this time?

Read **Colossians 2:8–12**

6) According to what you see in these verses, what might have been some of the heresy that had caused Paul to write this letter?

7) Finish the following sentence: "I would be fulfilled if…"

Spiritual math may well be a subject you never studied in school. Let me take a moment and share a brief spiritual formula with you.

$$(Christ) + (anything) = (Christ) - (something)$$

When it comes to our salvation in Christ, when we add anything it becomes subtraction. Paul understood this spiritual math and did not want anything to subtract from their understanding of the sufficiency of Christ.

8) What were the things that Paul was worried about being added to their salvation in Christ?

9) What statement does Paul make to remind them of the sufficiency of Christ?

The idea of the fullness of God's deity being found in human form was a direct attack on the teachings of the Gnostics. They believed that matter of any kind was evil. This certainly contradicts the creation account which tells us, *"God saw all that he had made, and it was very good. And there was evening, and there was morning—the sixth day."* **Genesis 1:31**

If matter was evil, then Jesus could not be true man and true God. Paul counters this heresy as he speaks of the fact that *"in Christ all the fullness of the Deity lives in bodily form."* **Colossians 2:9**

10) How does Paul connect us to the fullness of Christ?

11) Circumcision was an outward sign of obedience and connection to God. Read about it in Genesis 17:9-14. What does Paul mean when he says we have been circumcised in Christ?

12) What ideas, teachings, or philosophies are we faced with today that seek to add to our salvation equation?

13) How is it important today to be rooted in Christ? What comfort and encouragement do you take from these verses of Colossians today?

PRAYER
Jesus Christ, you are one with the Father and the Spirit in whom the complete fullness of God dwells, yet you chose to take on the fullness of man. I am humbled by this sacrifice as you bound yourself to us for all eternity. Help me to see in you the total and complete sacrifice for my sin. Help me to strive each day to grow deeper and stronger in my relationship with you and to be an example to those around me. Amen.

FOR NEXT WEEK
Read John 1:1–18 and 1 John 1:1–4 Imagine what it must have been like for John to spend time with Jesus—the one in whom all the fullness of the Deity lives in human form. Ponder your relationship with Christ and what it means for daily life to be rooted in Him.

MEMORY CHALLENGE
8See to it that no one takes you captive through hollow and deceptive philosophy, which depends on human tradition and the basic principles of this world rather than on Christ.
Colossians 2:8 (NIV)

6
SHADOWS AND FREEDOM

⁶ So then, just as you received Christ Jesus as Lord,
continue to live in him
Colossians 2:6

Shadows can really mess with your mind. Children's minds often go racing at the sight of a shadow. Shadows also can be a source of comfort. You can be delighted when a shadow announces the coming of someone you have been expecting.

In Colossians 2:17, Paul—speaking of the traditions and festivals passed down from Judaism—says, "these are shadows." The shadow allows us to see what is coming, but once the person comes into view for themselves, no one looks at the shadow.

God's covenant people were bound by the old covenant to many ceremonial and dietary rules. Leviticus 11 relates the food regulations and Leviticus 23 speaks of feasts and festivals.

Read *Colossians 2:13–17*

1) How did the Cross cancel the written code? (v. 13)

2) What was the purpose of these rules and regulations? Were they intended to be permanent rules for the spiritual life of God's people?

Read *Colossians 2:18–19* and *Hebrews 1*

3) What was the error from which Paul was leading them away in these verses?

Read *Colossians 2:20–13*

4) What was the error from which Paul was leading them away in these verses?

5) What "additions" to the faith are people tempted to use today?

6) Paul advises the Colossians to keep growing in their faith. What Christian leaders have helped you to continuing growing in your faith?

7) What does the phrase "fullness of Christ" mean to you?

Do you remember that great feeling of running out of school on the last day of the year? The amazing sense of freedom we had, free from homework and school rules? For many of us, those days may seem a million miles away, but we still enjoy our freedom.

If you don't believe that we enjoy our freedom, just look at the traffic on a Friday night in the summer as people head to their cabins or lake homes.

8) Why do we so enjoy the "end of the school year" freedom?

Read again *Colossians 2:13–23*

9) Paul is describing for the Colossians what might be called Christian freedom. How would you see these verses as a call to freedom?

10) Write a definition of Christian freedom.

11) How is "Christian freedom" often misused in our world?

12) This week, how can you best exercise your Christian freedom?

PRAYER

Help us to see, Father, that the shadow of the law and the prophets has been made clear and fulfilled in the life of your son, Jesus. Remind us of the great cost Jesus paid for our freedom. Help us to daily live out our Christian freedom as we strive to know more and more about our Savior Jesus, the Christ. Amen.

FOR NEXT WEEK

Read Colossians 3:1–11. Honestly think about how you deal with change. Are you a "go with the flow" kind of person, or do you like to "drop anchor" from time to time? Be prepared to share your thoughts on change next week.

MEMORY CHALLENGE

[13] When you were dead in your sins and in the uncircumcision of your sinful nature, God made you alive with Christ. He forgave us all our sins
Colossians 2:13 (NIV)

7
LOOK UP

¹ Since, then, you have been raised with Christ,
set your hearts on things above,
where Christ is seated
at the right hand of God.
Colossians 3:1 (NIV)

Several times in my life, I have been in a crowd with a friend. We point up to the sky and make it look like we are looking at something interesting. In reality, we are looking at nothing in particular. What happens next is always the same: the people around us who are watching us point and stare, start doing the same thing.

1) Have you ever done this? Why do other people stop and start looking up at the sky?

2) What does this tell us about our daily witness?

If you've never tried this, I suggest after Bible class heading out somewhere with a friend and pointing up. Perhaps you can even shade your eyes, or move over to the other person's spot to get the "correct" vantage point. Watch and see if others join you. Trust me . . . they will.

Read *Colossians 3:1–4*

Paul, in our text today, tells us to look up. He's not just pointing at nothing. He's calling us to change our perspective. He's calling us to take on our new life in Christ.

3) What does it mean to you to be "raised with Christ"?

4) What does it mean when someone says, "Set your sights higher"?

5) What difference does it make in your life to know that Christ is seated at the right hand of God?

Read *Colossians 3:5–9*

6) What do the items in the "put to death" list have in common? (v. 5)

7) Why is it important to the Colossians for Paul to add the comment about the "wrath of God"? (v. 6) Why is it important for us today?

Read *Romans 1:18–20*

8) Together with Colossians 3:6, what do we know about God's attitude toward sin? Is His attitude different toward the sin of a Christian?

9) What can we do to help keep God's perspective in mind on subjects like immorality and greed, when our culture accepts them as the norm?

I know if we searched your closet we might find that well-loved sweater, or pair of shoes that your spouse has been trying to get you to throw away for years. Why don't you? Because it is comfortable, familiar, and it is something you are accustomed to.

But the day will come when our favorite article of clothing gets replaced. It seems to take forever to get the new item "broken in." I will deny this to my wife, but often I am, in the long run, pleased with the new item (and many times even favor it over what I was previously using).

Paul calls us to put away the old, familiar, comfortable, and rotting. Paul calls us to new life.

10) Take a moment and complete the following statements:

I would like less of_____in my life.

I would like more of_____in my life.

Read *Colossians 3:8–11*

11) What does Paul say is being renewed in our new self? (v. 9)

12) What other resource does Paul list to help us in our transformation? (v. 11)

Read *Colossians 3:12–17*

13) What does Paul call the Colossians, and us, in verse 12? How does this compare to the "earthly nature" listed in verses 5–9?

14) What piece of Christ's clothing do you need to put on most today? (vs. 12–14)

15) Why does Paul remind us we are all one body?

16) What does it look like to "let the Word of Christ dwell in you richly?" (v. 16)

17) List the 3 biggest tasks that are on your agenda for today or tomorrow.

18) "Do it all in the name of the Lord Jesus"—how does this apply to the three items listed above?

19) How does worship play a role in this "new life"?

PRAYER

Lord, help us to clothe ourselves in the image and knowledge of Christ. Remind us of our newness in you, and the amazing power given to us for this change. Help us to encourage and challenge the whole body of Christ to live in you, and fill our hearts and lips with words of gratitude. Amen.

FOR NEXT WEEK

Find a hymn or Christian song that you can sing in the shower, or on the drive to work. Now sing it—make a joyful noise unto the Lord with gratitude. Share your song choice with the group next week. (We won't MAKE you sing it!)

MEMORY CHALLENGE

15 Let the peace of Christ rule in your hearts,
since as members of one body you were called to peace.
And be thankful.
16 Let the word of Christ dwell in you richly
as you teach and admonish one another with all wisdom,
and as you sing psalms, hymns and spiritual songs
with gratitude in your hearts to God.
Colossians 3:15–16 (NIV)

8
HOME AND AWAY

23 Whatever you do, work at it with all your heart,
as working for the Lord, not for men
Colossians 3:23

The third chapter of Colossians opens with Paul's call to holy living. He calls us to take off the old self and to put on the new life Christ has given us. Now, in the close of chapter 3, he breaks down what holy living looks like at home and away.

Paul opens this section with a word to families. He speaks to husbands and wives, as well as children. The nuclear family of Colossians is in many ways a far cry from the family of the 21st century. Yet, the desire and design of family has not changed.

1) As you think about your family of origin, what is your fondest childhood memory?

2) What attitudes or activities today do you think would be the mark of a Christian family?

Read *Colossians 3:12–21*

3) How are these two sections (vs. 12–17) and (vs. 18–21) tied together?

4) What does it mean for a wife to submit to her husband? What qualifier does Paul put on this submission? (v. 18)

5) What does it mean for a husband to love his wife? Why does Paul ask them not to be harsh?

Read *Ephesians 5:22–24*

6) How does this clarify our understanding of a wife's submission to her husband?

Read *Ephesians 5:25–33*

7) How does this clarify our understanding of a husband's love for his wife?

Read *Colossians 3:20–21* and *Ephesians 6:1–4*

8) Describe the relationship Paul seeks between a child and his/her parents?

9) How does this differ from the relationship many parents seek for their children?

10) What is the significance of Paul addressing children? What does this say about their role in the church?

The story is told of a factory in the Philippines that, for many months, had a Bible study that met over the lunch hour. One day, the supervisor of the factory came to the leader of the study and asked, "Could you start some more Bible studies in our factory?" When asked why the sudden interest, the supervisor replied, "The men in the study have become my best workers."

This would not have surprised Paul in the least. Paul continues to encourage workers to give their best at all times.

11) What behavior would you hope to see in the life of a Christian at work?

Read *Colossians 3:22–4:1*

12) What instructions does Paul give to slaves?

13) What instructions does Paul give to masters?

14) What gospel motivation does Paul give to slaves and to masters? (4:1)

15) How could following these instructions change how you do your job, whether as an employee or as an employer?

Read *Colossians 2:9–10, 3:23–24*

16) How do these verses impact our view of life at home and away?

17) What changes can you make in your life this week to reflect Paul's advice about life as a Christian at home and at work?

PRAYER

Lord, you call us your chosen people, holy and dearly loved. Help us to reflect who you see in us to those in our family and at our job. We rejoice that you are over us and in us as we live this new life. Help us to live a life that demands an explanation. Grant us words to share the story of your Lordship in our lives. Lord Jesus, help us to know you more and more each day. Amen.

FOR NEXT WEEK

As we prepare to close this study of Colossians, re-read the entire book, listening for the voice of a caring pastor as he speaks to a church he loves.

MEMORY CHALLENGE

23 Whatever you do, work at it with all your heart, as working for the Lord, not for men,
24 since you know that you will receive an inheritance from the Lord as a reward. It is the Lord Christ you are serving.
Colossians 3:23–24

9
PRAY FOR THE FAMILY

² Devote yourselves to prayer, being watchful and thankful.
Colossians 4:2

The last portion of Paul's letter is filled with personal notes, encouragement, and greetings. As we look at this final section, we get a glimpse into the early church. We meet some of the key people and, as we look at their backgrounds, we find out about the conditions that helped the church to grow.

If you were an original Colossian church member, you would know many of the names Paul lists here. Our goal is to help you begin to hear these words fresh and full of context and meaning so you can pass on their richness to the church today.

Read *Colossians 4:2–6*

1) If you had to summarize this section in one word, what word would you choose?

2) How does Paul call them to support him as he ministers in Rome? (vs. 3–4)

3) What does Paul say about their opportunities to share the gospel of Christ? (v. 5)

4) What does he say about the way they should speak? (v.6)

5) What do these last two questions say to us today?

6) What does it take to "know how to answer everyone"?

7) Are there theological questions or topics you try to stay away from? If so, what might those topics be?

Now let's meet some of the people and explore some of the places to help us better understand this last section of Colossians.

Tychicus: An associate and friend of Paul's, believed to be from Ephesus. Because he had been chosen by the churches of Asia Minor to carry the money collected for the Christians in need to Jerusalem, it is assumed that he traveled to Jerusalem with Paul. Paul sent him with letters Paul had written to the churches in Colossae and Ephesus.

Onesimus: Onésimus was a slave who ran away from his master, Philemon—a friend of Paul's from Colossae. Onesimus also became a close friend of Paul's while in Rome. It was while spending time in Rome with Paul that Onesimus became a Christian. He, too, carried the letter from Paul to the church at Colossae.

Read *Colossians 4:7–9*

8) What is the purpose for sending Tychicus to Colossae? (vs. 7–8)

9) What would you hope someone would say about you if they wrote a note of introduction for you?

10) How do Paul's words help to smooth the path for Onesimus' return to Colossae?

Aristarchus: A Macedonian of Thessalonica who traveled with Paul on his third missionary journey through Asia Minor. A faithful companion and friend, Aristarchus accompanied Paul to Rome. He attended to Paul and shared his imprisonment, and was identified as a "fellow prisoner."

The phrase that Paul introduces here, "fellow prisoner," does not indicate they are being held by Rome. This designation was given to those who were being held by the gospel and were choosing to remain and serve Paul's needs in Rome.

Mark: John Mark was the cousin of Barnabas, and friend and companion of Peter and Paul. His mother Mary was an influential woman in the church of Jerusalem. She possessed a large house with servants that was used for meetings of the early church.

Mark traveled with Barnabas and Paul on their first missionary journey as far as Perga. He served as an assistant. Most likely this involved cooking and making arrangements for their travel. In Perga, Mark left the journey for an unknown reason.

Mark is best known for writing the Gospel of Mark. Mark's lasting impression on the church comes from his writing. He was the first to develop the literary form known as the Gospel.

Jesus Justus: A Jewish Christian and co-worker of Paul who sent greetings to the church at Colossae. His Jewish name was Jesus, and his Roman name was Justus.

Read *Colossians 4:10–11*

11) What is unique about Mark and Justus? How might this be significant to the Colossians?

Epaphras: A Christian preacher who founded the church at Colossae. Epaphras brought news of the church at Colossae to Paul while he was in Rome. This prompted Paul to write the letter we have been studying to the church at Colossae. Epaphras stayed on with Paul in Rome and became a "fellow prisoner." (Philemon 23)

Laodicea: A present-day city in the Lycus Valley of Turkey. A Roman province of Asia in New Testament times. This letter was intended for the church at Laodicea as well. Most believe this church was started by Paul when he spent time living in Ephesus.

Hierapolis: A Roman city near Colossae, it is now known as Pamukkale in modern Turkey. The hot springs of Hierapolis have, over the centuries, petrified into an amazing waterfall of stone.

12) What does Epaphras, who serves as a "fellow prisoner" with Paul, do on behalf of his church at Colossae?

Read *Colossians 4:12–13*

Luke: The author of the Gospel of Luke and the Acts of the Apostles. Luke was a physician and may very well have been a slave at one time. Many people who became physicians were slaves trained in medicine to serve the family of the master. Luke was a Gentile and the only non-Jewish author of a New Testament book.

Luke was a friend of Paul and traveled with him on some of his missionary journeys. He sailed to Rome with Paul and stayed with him there.

Demas: A Christian who spent time with Paul during his Roman imprisonment. During Paul's time in Rome, Demas deserted Paul, "having loved this present world" (2 Timothy 4:10), and went off to Thessalonica.

Nympha: A Christian woman of Laodicea or Colossae who opened her home as a gathering place for the Christians of the area.

Archippus: A Christian in Colossae who held an official position in the church. Paul describes him as a "fellow soldier" and calls on him to fulfill his ministry in the Lord. Tradition lists Archippus as the son of Philemon.

Read *Colossians 4:14–18*

13) Paul demonstrated the value of teamwork in ministry. How well do you work with other Christians for the kingdom of God?

14) Most letters were written by scribes during the days of the New Testament. It was customary for Paul to write the final words of a letter in his own hand. Looking at the final verse of this letter, what impact might these words have had on his audience?

Bringing this study to a close, take a few moments to reflect on the following questions.

15) Looking back over the book of Colossians, what section was the most meaningful to you personally?

16) What have you learned and how might you apply those lessons to your life?

17) Based on what you have learned in this study, how would you compare the Christian church of Paul's time with the church today? Were there more problems and challenges then or now?

18) Would you have liked being a part of the early church, such as the Colossian church? Why or why not?

PRAYER

Lord, keep us wise in the ways that we interact with all those who cross our path. Let our words and actions be full of grace and reflect the new life you have given to us. Help us to be prepared to give an answer to everyone about the hope inside of us, and keep us open to the opportunities to speak of you each day. Grant us the wisdom to apply what we have learned in these lessons, and the desire to help lead someone else to know you more through the lessons of Colossians. In the name of Christ who is sovereign and supreme over all things, yet delights to know us by name, Amen.

WHAT'S NEXT

As we close the book of Colossians, read through it one more time with a notecard or journal near you. Copy your favorite sections of the letter onto cards or journal pages, which you can use as the basis for daily meditation and prayer in the coming weeks. I also want to encourage you to share your answers to questions 14 and 15 from this study with a friend or family member. Invite them to study the book with you and share what you have learned.

MEMORY CHALLENGE

⁵ Be wise in the way you act toward outsiders;
make the most of every opportunity.
⁶ Let your conversation be always full of grace,
seasoned with salt, so that you may know how to answer everyone.
Colossians 4:5–6 (NIV)

10
LEADER'S GUIDE

Let me start by saying thank you! Thanks for taking the time to serve as the leader of this study. Your role is important in the success of this study. On the following pages you will find a few "Bible Study Leadership Tips" to help you lead this or any study more effectively.

When I wrote the study, I fully knew what I meant by each and every question—they all made perfect sense to me. You, unfortunately, do not have the benefit of knowing what I was thinking when I wrote this study. With this in mind, we have developed study-by-study leader's notes.

These notes are not included with this book; we are hosting them online. The reason for this is our deep desire to keep the content fresh by adding additional resources for you to use. We also want to share ideas as we receive them from others like you, who have led this study with their group. To view this content, visit our website at:

http://craigmccourt.com/kc-leadersguide/

Bible Study Leadership Tips

PREPARATION

Prayer is the best way to start your preparation each week. Next, make sure you have taken the time to work through the study yourself, reading through any leader's notes provided (on our website). Make notes of your thoughts in your study guide as you prepare. Make note of any additional text you wish to use that is not listed in the material.

Without preparation, we can easily give too much time to the early questions in the study, which doesn't leave us with enough time to work our way through all that we hoped to cover. In your preparation, mark the key questions and topics you want to make sure to cover.

BEGIN ON TIME

One of our greatest issues when leading a Bible study is time. It is a finite resource, and your students have committed to a set starting and ending time. While it is important to allow students to greet each other and catch up on their lives, try to allow time "pre-study time" for this (i.e., meet at 6:30 with the study beginning at 7:00 and ending at 8:00).

When the study does not start when promised, two things happen. The first is very simple: you run the risk of running out of time to complete the lesson. The second is the snowball effect. This is where students know you don't start on time, so they don't show up on time. This issue snowballs until those who are good about getting there on time stop coming out of sheer frustration.

If you establish a culture of starting on time, regardless of whether or not everyone in the group has arrived, and not allowing latecomers to interrupt your discussion when they arrive, you will find that group members become more punctual.

END ON TIME

Okay, so you probably know where this one is going. Just as critical to getting a good start is getting a good end. If you do not honor the time commitments that the group has agreed to, it becomes a source of frustration. When this happens, students leave class not remembering the lesson of the day, but remembering how they felt about class running over.

PRAYER REQUESTS

There is something meaningful in a small group sharing life together by taking time to include the sharing of prayer requests. However, we also know that sometimes sharing requests can easily turn into story time as people want to fill in back story on their requests. This in turn often opens the door for lengthy discussions as other members offer advice or input.

There are two ways you can deal with this issue. The first is to simple figure in time to allow for this conversation. This might mean ending the study time 15 minutes early to allow for the prayer requests. A better way perhaps might be to provide note cards for people to write down their requests and share them at the end or simply have members swap cards with someone else.

THE MAIN THING

It can be a lot of work to keep the main thing, the main thing. In this case, the main thing is The Word. There are any number of reasons why people choose to attend a particular Bible study. They also come with varying biblical background and interest. It can be easy for your group to slip from being a Bible study group into becoming more of a personal support group. Trying to find that right balance between biblical study and personal support is a significant challenge for every small-group leader.

As group members become more comfortable with one another, they become more comfortable in what they share with the group. Times may even arise when, due to a personal need of a member, the idea of setting aside the study to use that time to listen, advise, and encourage might become an issue. While I don't want to say this should never be done, I want to advise against using your regular time for this.

God has promised that His word is living and active. The Word of God speaks into every need and situation in our lives. It heals, it gives perspective, it instructs, convicts, restores, and renews. Please do not assume that the advice and discussion of the group has more power than your discussion of the truths of God's Word to help that hurting person.

IS THAT COFFEE I SMELL?

There is nothing like a cup of coffee and a few goodies to help a study move along. I am a firm believer in a little food fellowship with Bible study. I have yet to be in a small group study where someone does not have a desire to help provide or arrange for goodies. Don't let this tip seem trite as compared to the rest—and if it does, think it over again with a cup of coffee and a Danish!

ABOUT THE AUTHOR

For more than 25 years, Craig McCourt has ministered full-time to youth and their families, using his remarkable teaching style to present biblical truths in ways that motivate change in believers' lives. He is the founder of Pondering God Ministries, and the creator of the blog Pondering God.

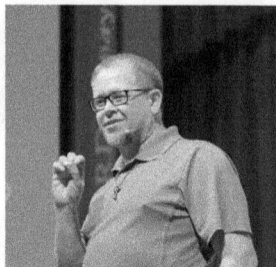

Craig's first book, *Pondering God—Seeing God in Everyday Life*, is available through his website or from Amazon and Barnes & Noble. He also hosts a weekly podcast called *Pondering God: with Craig McCourt*. You can listen online to current and classic episodes, as well as subscribe to the podcast at www.CraigMcCourt.com.

Over the years, Craig has spoken to hundreds of groups, both large and small. He has been blessed to have the opportunity to speak internationally, as well as in many different places across the United States. Shirley, Craig's wife of 29 years, joins him as the Pondering God ministry grows. Shirley brings many years of camp and retreat experience to Pondering God, as well as a heart for ministering to women.

Shirley and Craig live in Eden Prairie, just outside of Minneapolis, Minnesota, and have two adult sons who also live near them.

The Pondering God mission: As Disciples of Christ, we seek to use the stories of Scripture and life to proclaim the works of God and ponder what He has done, encouraging and equipping others to do the same. For more on my speaking ministry visit **www.craigmccourt.com**

To KNOW CHRIST is to Serve
World Servants Mission Trips:
Everyone is Welcome

My wife and I have partnered with World Servants for many years. We invite you to discover the joy and power serving on a World Servants mission trip.

By going on a World Servants' mission trip, you can make a difference by strengthening families, engaging congregations, bringing hope to communities and giving God an opportunity to touch the lives of many.

World Servants' mission is to mobilize a global network of people to impact the world through Jesus Christ by responding to physical and spiritual needs AND to develop and facilitate life-changing learning and serving experiences that bring hope to the world.

A World Servants short-term mission is a weeklong experience for groups, families and individuals to assist in what God is doing in a specific community. The foundation of our ministry is to enter every relationship and experience with the attitude of a Learner, Servant and Storyteller. We hold to the value of learning about the community in which we serving, coming alongside those God is working through and demonstrating care and concern in a way that preserves dignity.

The mission is to meet both the physical and spiritual needs of our "neighbors" through acts of service, i.e.

construction, rebuilding projects, painting tasks, and yard upkeep, as well as ministry outreach activities such as Kids' Club, Sports Camp, women's ministry, home visits, community worship and gatherings.

Trip participant needs are taken care of as World Servants provides food, housing, transportation, construction and ministry materials, t-shirt, journal and World Servants trip facilitators who have long-term relationships with community leaders. Each evening a World Servants mission leader will guide the group through a reflection process, while challenging the group to continue a life of service.

All our mission experiences are designed to have a long-term impact. Families value experiences which incorporate the whole family, to be a part of a physical experience of hands-on, face to face interactions with people where their presence and service makes a difference that is directly felt, seen and heard. A comment often heard is, *"This was a defining moment in my life and in the life of our family. We will never be the same."*

world servants
30
years of serving
est. 1986

*To learn about World Servants' life-changing mission trips, please visit our website: **www.worldservants.org** or contact World Servants at 612-866-0010.*

OTHER RESOURCES

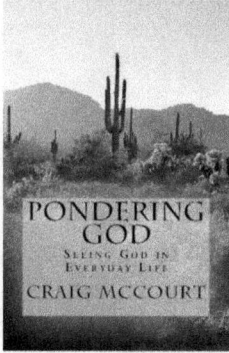

Looking for a little inspiration for the day? Want a devotional to start your next church meeting? This book may be just what you are looking for. Pondering God is a collection of stories, sometimes humorous, always designed to help you see God in everyday life. These stories are filled with scripture and contain a question designed to get you Pondering God.

This retreat, which could also be used as a series of 6-8 Bible studies, tries to get at some of these deeper meanings of Ephesians 3:16-17. If Christ dwells in us, that means that our bodies are His home. He lives here. By taking a look at different rooms in this "home" we begin to understand more fully how these verses impact our lives. It is based on a pamphlet by Robert Munger by the same name. This retreat package includes everything you need for your Bible Study portion of a Women's Retreat and includes some ideas for games, quiet times, music, and other program areas of your retreat.

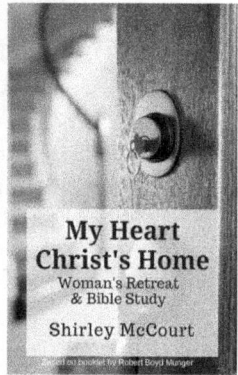

To purchase these and other resources visit:

www.GodPondersPublishing.com

PONDERING GOD

WITH AUTHOR & SPEAKER CRAIG McCOURT

Subscribe to Craig's weekly podcast visit

www.craigmccourt.com/podcast

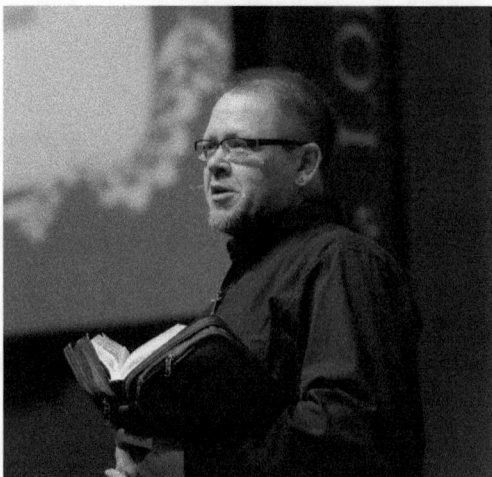

Why not invite Craig to speak at your next conference, retreat or event.

Craig is also available for ministry consultations and training events.

For a complete list of topics and more information on the speaking ministry of Craig McCourt visit:

CRAIG MCCOURT.COM

WHAT OTHERS SAY

Craig's unique ability to bring God's word into how we live our lives and make it so easy to apply has truly encouraged me. He is not shy about sharing his own faith journey and that makes his messages that much more real and inspiring.
Rick, Retreat Participant

If you are looking for a Christian speaker, teacher or a leader for a retreat, Craig is the one to hire! His natural caring spirit and ability to break down God's Word is refreshing and engaging for the listener. Craig's humble spirit pours out onto you and you can't help but want what Craig has!
Jana, Event Participant

Craig's teaching is engaging for young and old alike. He has a unique ability to teach God's word in a way that is down to earth, clear and relevant for today. His sense of humor brings lots of laughter and fun, making the time spent enjoyable and memorable.
Jason, Bible Class Participant

"This guy is a funny, funny man"
Rev. Dr. Jeffery Schrank – Christ Church Lutheran
- Pheonix AZ

"I have seen God use Craig through engaging his audience by bringing God's Word to meet them where they are at BUT no one leaves without their lives transformed by the power of the Holy Spirit."
Traci Kohls - Adjunct Faculty at
Concordia University St. Paul

"Craig McCourt is one of the most inspiring, yet down-to-earth speakers I have ever had the opportunity to listen to. His God-given talents are many. I particularly like the fact that Craig is extremely effective in motivating and uplifting people of all age groups--teens, parents, seniors--with his love for the Lord. "
Dr. James Pingel - Secondary Education Department Chair -
Concordia University Wisconsin